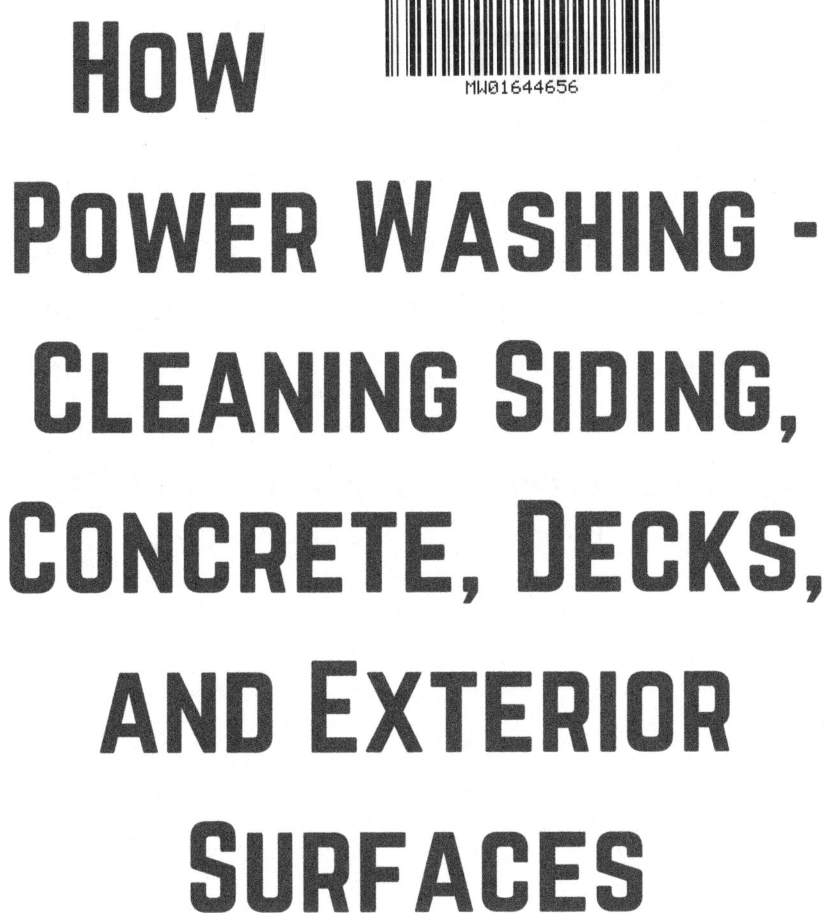

How Power Washing - Cleaning Siding, Concrete, Decks, and Exterior Surfaces

The Ultimate Guide to Efficient and Effective Power Washing Techniques for Transforming Your Home's Exterior

The Fix It Guy

Table of Contents

Introduction

Hey there, homeowner! Are you tired of looking at your dingy, grimy exterior surfaces and feeling a bit embarrassed about your home's curb appeal? Trust me, I've been there. It's easy to let the years of dirt, grime, and weather take their toll on your siding, concrete, decks, and more. But here's the good news: you have the power to transform your home's exterior and make it look like new again!

That's where power washing comes in. It's like a magic wand for your home's exterior surfaces. With the right techniques and equipment, you can blast away years of buildup and reveal the true beauty of your home. And let me tell you, the satisfaction of seeing your surfaces sparkle and shine is unbeatable.

But power washing isn't just about aesthetics. Regular power washing can actually protect your home from damage caused by dirt, mold, and mildew. It can extend the life of your siding, concrete, and decks, saving you money on costly repairs down the line. Plus, it's a great way to boost your home's value if you're looking to sell.

Now, I know what you might be thinking. "Power washing seems intimidating. I don't want to damage my surfaces or hurt myself in the process." I hear you. That's why I've put together this comprehensive guide to power washing. I'll walk you through the process step-by-step, from choosing the right equipment to tackling tough stains. And of course, I'll cover all the safety precautions you need to take to protect yourself and your home.

So, whether you're a power washing newbie or a seasoned pro, this book has something for you. We'll cover everything from basic techniques to advanced applications, so you can take your power washing skills to the next level.

And by the end of this book, you'll have the confidence and know-how to tackle any power washing project that comes your way.

So what are you waiting for? Let's dive in and start transforming your home's exterior today! Get ready to impress your neighbors, boost your home's value, and most importantly, feel proud of the place you call home. Trust me, the power of power washing is real, and it's time for you to harness it.

Chapter 1
Preparing for Power Washing

Assessing Your Exterior Surfaces

Before you dive into power washing your home's exterior, it's crucial to take the time to properly prepare. One of the most important steps in this preparation process is assessing your exterior surfaces. By taking a thorough look at the surfaces you plan to clean, you can ensure that you're using the right equipment, cleaning solutions, and techniques for the job.

Assessing Your Exterior Surfaces

The first step in assessing your exterior surfaces is to take a walk around your home and identify the different types of surfaces you'll be cleaning. This might include siding (such as vinyl, wood, or fiber cement), concrete (such as driveways, sidewalks, or patios), decks and fences (made of wood or composite materials), roofs (such as asphalt shingles or tiles), and masonry (like brick, stone, or stucco).

As you identify these surfaces, take note of their current condition. Are there any areas that are particularly dirty or stained? Are there any signs of damage, such as cracks, chips, or rot? These are important factors to consider when deciding on your cleaning approach.

For example, if you have a wood deck that's showing signs of wear and tear, you'll want to be extra careful when power washing to avoid causing further damage. This might mean using a lower pressure setting on your power washer, or even opting for a gentler cleaning method altogether.

On the other hand, if you have a concrete driveway with tough oil stains, you might need to use a higher pressure setting and a specialized cleaning solution to get the job done.

In addition to identifying the types of surfaces and their condition, you'll also want to take note of any obstacles or hazards in the area. This might include plants, outdoor furniture, or electrical outlets that need to be protected during the cleaning process.

Once you've thoroughly assessed your exterior surfaces, you can start to plan your power washing approach. This might involve researching the best cleaning solutions and equipment for your specific surfaces, as well as gathering any necessary safety gear (like gloves, goggles, and ear protection).

It's also a good idea to do a spot test in an inconspicuous area before tackling the entire surface. This will allow you to gauge the effectiveness of your cleaning solution and pressure setting, and make any necessary adjustments before moving forward.

By taking the time to properly assess your exterior surfaces, you can ensure that your power washing project goes smoothly and effectively. You'll be able to target your cleaning efforts where they're needed most, while also protecting your surfaces from potential damage.

In the following sections, we'll delve deeper into the specific steps involved in preparing for power washing, including choosing the right equipment and cleaning solutions, and protecting your landscaping and surrounding areas. But by starting with a thorough assessment of your exterior surfaces, you'll be setting yourself up for success from the very beginning.

Safety Precautions and Equipment

Power washing can be an incredibly effective way to clean your home's exterior surfaces, but it's important to remember that it involves working with high-pressure water and potentially harmful cleaning solutions. To ensure a safe and successful power washing experience, it's crucial to take the necessary safety precautions and use the appropriate equipment.

Safety Precautions

Before you begin power washing, there are several safety precautions you should take to protect yourself and others around you:

1. Wear protective gear: This includes safety goggles to protect your eyes from flying debris, gloves to protect your hands from cleaning solutions, and ear protection to guard against the loud noise of the power washer. If you're working with particularly harsh chemicals, you may also want to wear a respirator mask.

2. Clear the area: Make sure the area you'll be working in is clear of any obstacles or hazards, such as electrical outlets, loose wires, or fragile objects. If you're working near windows, make sure they're closed and locked to prevent water from getting inside.

3. Keep children and pets away: Power washing can be dangerous, so it's important to keep children and pets at a safe distance while you work. If possible, have someone else supervise them while you're power washing to ensure they stay out of harm's way.

4. Test your equipment: Before you start power washing, test your equipment to make sure it's working properly. This includes checking for leaks, testing the pressure settings, and making sure the nozzle is securely attached.

5. Use caution with cleaning solutions: If you're using any cleaning solutions in your power washing, be sure to read and follow the manufacturer's instructions carefully. Some solutions can be harmful if ingested or inhaled, so it's important to use them in a well-ventilated area and avoid getting them on your skin or in your eyes.

Equipment

Having the right equipment is essential for a safe and effective power washing experience. Here are some of the key pieces of equipment you'll need:

1. Power washer: Of course, the most important piece of equipment for power washing is the power washer itself. There are many different types and models available, so it's important to choose one that's appropriate for your needs. Consider factors like the pressure rating (measured in PSI), flow rate (measured in GPM), and nozzle options when making your selection.

2. Nozzles: Different nozzles can be used to adjust the pressure and spray pattern of the water coming out of your power washer. Most power washers come with a variety of nozzles, including a low-pressure nozzle for gentle cleaning and a high-pressure nozzle for tougher stains.

3. Extension wand: An extension wand can be attached to your power washer to help you reach high or hard-to-reach areas, such as second-story windows or gutters.

4. Cleaning solutions: Depending on the type of surface you're cleaning and the level of grime, you may need to use a cleaning solution in addition to water. Be sure to choose a solution that's appropriate for your specific surface and follow the manufacturer's instructions for use.

5. Safety gear: As mentioned above, protective gear like safety goggles, gloves, ear protection, and a respirator mask are essential for safe power washing.

By taking the necessary safety precautions and using the appropriate equipment, you can ensure a safe and effective power washing experience. Remember to always prioritize safety and take your time to ensure the best possible results. With the right approach and equipment, you'll be able to transform your home's exterior surfaces and enjoy a cleaner, more beautiful living space.

Choosing the Right Power Washer

When it comes to power washing your home's exterior surfaces, having the right equipment is key. And the most important piece of equipment in your power washing arsenal is, of course, the power washer itself. But with so many different types and models available on the market, how do you choose the right one for your needs? Let's break it down.

Types of Power Washers

There are two main types of power washers: electric and gas-powered. Electric power washers are typically less powerful than gas-powered models, with a pressure range of 1,300 to 2,000 PSI (pounds per square inch). They're best suited for smaller, lighter-duty tasks like cleaning patio furniture, grills, and cars.

Gas-powered power washers, on the other hand, pack a bigger punch, with a pressure range of 2,000 to 4,000 PSI or higher. They're ideal for tackling tougher jobs like stripping paint, removing stubborn stains from concrete, and cleaning large surface areas like driveways and decks.

Factors to Consider

When choosing a power washer, there are several key factors to consider:

1. Pressure rating (PSI): The pressure rating tells you how much force the water will have when it comes out of the power washer. Higher PSI means more cleaning power, but it also means a higher risk of damage to softer surfaces like wood or vinyl siding. As a general rule, a pressure rating of 2,000 to 3,000 PSI is sufficient for most home exterior cleaning tasks.

2. Flow rate (GPM): The flow rate, measured in gallons per minute (GPM), tells you how much water the power washer uses. A higher GPM means faster cleaning, but it also means you'll use more water. A flow rate of 2 to 4 GPM is typical for most residential power washers.

3. Nozzle options: Different nozzles can be used to adjust the pressure and spray pattern of the water coming out of your power washer. Look for a model that comes with a variety of nozzle options, including a low-pressure nozzle for gentle cleaning and a high-pressure nozzle for tougher stains.

4. Portability: If you plan on moving your power washer around a lot, look for a model with wheels and a sturdy handle for easy transport. Some models even come with built-in detergent tanks for added convenience.

5. Noise level: Gas-powered power washers tend to be louder than electric models, so if noise is a concern, an electric model may be a better choice.

6. Price: Power washers can range in price from around $100 for a basic electric model to $1,000 or more for a high-end gas-powered model. Consider your budget and the frequency with which you plan to use your power washer when making your decision.

Making Your Selection

Once you've considered these factors, it's time to start shopping around. Read reviews from other homeowners and professionals to get a sense of which models are the most reliable and effective. Look for a model with a good warranty and customer support, in case you run into any issues down the line.

If you're still unsure which model to choose, consider renting a power washer from a local hardware store or home improvement center before making a purchase. This will give you a chance to try out different models and see which one works best for your needs.

Ultimately, the right power washer for you will depend on your specific cleaning needs, budget, and personal preferences. By taking the time to carefully consider your options and do your research, you can find a model that will help you achieve the best possible results for your home's exterior surfaces.

Selecting Appropriate Cleaning Solutions

While a power washer's high-pressure water spray can work wonders on its own, sometimes you need a little extra cleaning power to tackle stubborn stains and buildup. That's where cleaning solutions come in. But with so many different types of solutions available, how do you know which one to choose? Let's take a closer look.

Types of Cleaning Solutions

There are several different types of cleaning solutions that can be used with a power washer, each designed for specific surfaces and types of grime. Some of the most common types include:

1. All-purpose cleaners: These versatile cleaners can be used on a variety of surfaces, including vinyl siding, brick, and concrete. They're effective at removing dirt, grime, and light stains.

2. Degreasers: As the name suggests, degreasers are designed to break down and remove grease and oil stains. They're often used on driveways, garage floors, and other surfaces that are prone to oil and grease buildup.

3. Mildew removers: Mildew can be a stubborn problem on exterior surfaces, particularly in damp or shady areas. Mildew removers are specially formulated to kill mildew and prevent it from returning.

4. Deck and fence cleaners: These cleaners are designed specifically for use on wooden decks and fences. They often contain brighteners to help restore the wood's natural color and prevent future graying.

5. Roof cleaners: Roof cleaners are formulated to remove algae, moss, and other stains from roofing materials like asphalt shingles and tiles.

Factors to Consider

When selecting a cleaning solution, there are several key factors to consider:

1. Surface type: Make sure to choose a cleaning solution that's appropriate for the surface you'll be cleaning. Using the wrong type of cleaner can damage or discolor certain surfaces.

2. Environmental impact: Some cleaning solutions contain harsh chemicals that can be harmful to the environment. Look for eco-friendly options that are biodegradable and free of toxic chemicals.

3. Safety: Always read the manufacturer's instructions and safety precautions before using any cleaning solution. Some solutions can be harmful if ingested or inhaled, so it's important to use them in a well-ventilated area and wear protective gear like gloves and goggles.

4. Concentration: Some cleaning solutions come in concentrated form and need to be diluted with water before use. Others are ready to use right out of the bottle. Consider your needs and preferences when deciding which type to choose.

5. Price: Cleaning solutions can vary widely in price, from a few dollars for a basic all-purpose cleaner to $50 or more for a specialized roof cleaner. Consider your budget and the frequency with which you plan to use the cleaner when making your selection.

Application Methods

Once you've selected the appropriate cleaning solution for your needs, it's important to apply it correctly for best results. There are two main methods for applying cleaning solutions with a power washer:

1. Downstream injection: With this method, the cleaning solution is mixed with the water in the power washer's pump and sprayed onto the surface through the nozzle. This method is convenient and efficient, but it can be more difficult to control the concentration of the cleaning solution.

2. Upstream injection: With this method, the cleaning solution is added to a separate container that's connected to the power washer's intake hose. The solution is then drawn into the machine and mixed with the water before being sprayed onto the surface. This method allows for more precise control over the concentration of the cleaning solution.

Whichever method you choose, be sure to follow the manufacturer's instructions for mixing and applying the cleaning solution. Some solutions may need to be left on the surface for a certain amount of time before being rinsed off, while others can be rinsed immediately.

By selecting the appropriate cleaning solution and applying it correctly, you can achieve the best possible results for your power washing project. Just remember to always prioritize safety and follow the manufacturer's instructions carefully to avoid damaging your surfaces or harming the environment.

Protecting Your Landscape and Surroundings

While power washing can be a highly effective way to clean and maintain your home's exterior surfaces, it's important to remember that the high-pressure water spray can also cause damage to your landscape and surroundings if you're not careful. To ensure a safe and successful power washing experience, it's crucial to take steps to protect your plants, outdoor structures, and other nearby areas.

Assessing Your Surroundings

Before you begin power washing, take a walk around your property and assess your surroundings. Look for any fragile or delicate plants, outdoor furniture, or decorative elements that could be damaged by the high-pressure water spray. Make note of any electrical outlets, light fixtures, or other sensitive areas that need to be protected.

If you have any doubt about whether an item can withstand the force of the power washer, it's best to err on the side of caution and move it out of the way or cover it with a tarp or plastic sheeting.

Protecting Your Plants

One of the most important things to consider when power washing your home's exterior is the impact on your landscaping. While most plants can withstand some exposure to the power washer's spray, others may be more delicate and prone to damage.

To protect your plants, follow these tips:

1. Cover delicate plants: Use tarps, plastic sheeting, or even old bedsheets to cover any delicate plants or shrubs that are in the path of the power washer's spray. Make sure the coverings are secure and won't blow away in the wind.

2. Wet down your plants: Before you begin power washing, use a garden hose to wet down any nearby plants. This will help to prevent them from absorbing too much of the cleaning solution and will also help to rinse away any overspray.

3. Avoid direct spraying: When power washing near plants, try to avoid spraying them directly with the high-pressure water. Instead, aim the spray away from the plants and let the overspray fall onto them gently.

4. Rinse thoroughly: After power washing, make sure to rinse any nearby plants thoroughly with clean water to remove any cleaning solution residue.

Protecting Other Surfaces

In addition to your plants, there are several other surfaces and structures around your home that may need protection during power washing:

1. Windows and doors: Make sure all windows and doors are closed and locked before power washing to prevent water from getting inside your home. If you're power washing near windows, use a low-pressure nozzle and keep the spray at least a foot away from the glass to avoid damage.

2. Outdoor furniture: Move any outdoor furniture, grills, or decorative elements out of the way before power washing. If you can't move them, cover them with tarps or plastic sheeting to protect them from the spray.

3. Electrical outlets and light fixtures: Cover any electrical outlets, light fixtures, or other sensitive areas with plastic sheeting and tape to prevent water from getting inside.

4. Air conditioners and vents: Avoid spraying directly into air conditioners, vents, or other openings in your home's exterior. The high-pressure water can damage the unit or force water and debris inside your home.

5. Neighboring properties: Be mindful of any overspray that may drift onto neighboring properties. Make sure to keep the spray contained to your own property and clean up any mess you may make.

By taking these steps to protect your landscape and surroundings, you can ensure a safe and effective power washing experience. Remember to always prioritize safety and take your time to avoid causing any unintended damage. With the right preparation and precautions, you can enjoy a beautifully cleaned home exterior without sacrificing the health and beauty of your landscaping.

Chapter 2
Power Washing Techniques for Different Surfaces

Siding: Vinyl, Wood, and Fiber Cement

When it comes to power washing your home's exterior, one of the most important areas to focus on is the siding. After all, your siding is what protects your home from the elements and plays a big role in its overall appearance. But with so many different types of siding materials available, it's important to know how to properly clean and maintain each one. In this chapter, we'll take a closer look at three of the most common types of siding: vinyl, wood, and fiber cement.

Vinyl Siding

Vinyl siding is one of the most popular siding materials on the market today, and for good reason. It's affordable, durable, and relatively low maintenance. However, it can still benefit from regular power washing to keep it looking its best.

When power washing vinyl siding, it's important to use a low-pressure setting and a wide-angle nozzle to avoid damaging the material. Start by wetting down the siding with plain water to remove any loose dirt and debris. Then, apply a gentle cleaning solution using a downstream injection method and let it sit for a few minutes to penetrate any stubborn stains.

Use a soft-bristled brush or a low-pressure nozzle to scrub the siding gently, working in small sections from the bottom up to avoid streaking. Rinse the siding thoroughly with plain water, making sure to remove all of the cleaning solution.

Wood Siding

Wood siding is a classic and timeless choice for many homeowners, but it does require a bit more maintenance than some other materials. Regular power washing can help to prevent rot, decay, and insect infestations, as well as keep the wood looking its best.

When power washing wood siding, it's important to use a low-pressure setting and a wide-angle nozzle to avoid damaging the wood fibers. Start by wetting down the siding with plain water to remove any loose dirt and debris. Then, apply a specialized wood cleaner using a downstream injection method and let it sit for a few minutes to penetrate any stubborn stains.

Use a soft-bristled brush or a low-pressure nozzle to scrub the siding gently, working in small sections from the bottom up to avoid streaking. Pay special attention to any areas that are prone to mold or mildew growth, such as shaded or damp spots.

Rinse the siding thoroughly with plain water, making sure to remove all of the cleaning solution. If the wood appears to be drying out or splintering after power washing, consider applying a wood sealer or stain to protect it from the elements.

Fiber Cement Siding

Fiber cement siding is a relatively new material that has become increasingly popular in recent years. It's made from a mixture of wood fibers, cement, and sand, and is known for its durability and resistance to fire, insects, and rot. However, like any other siding material, it can still benefit from regular power washing to keep it looking its best.

When power washing fiber cement siding, it's important to use a low-pressure setting and a wide-angle nozzle to avoid damaging the material. Start by wetting down the siding with plain water to remove any loose dirt and debris. Then, apply a gentle cleaning solution using a downstream injection method and let it sit for a few minutes to penetrate any stubborn stains.

Use a soft-bristled brush or a low-pressure nozzle to scrub the siding gently, working in small sections from the bottom up to avoid streaking. Pay special attention to any areas that are prone to mold or mildew growth, such as shaded or damp spots.

Rinse the siding thoroughly with plain water, making sure to remove all of the cleaning solution. If the fiber cement appears to be chalky or faded after power washing, consider applying a specialized masonry sealer to protect it from the elements.

By following these tips and techniques for power washing your home's siding, you can keep it looking its best for years to come. Just remember to always prioritize safety and take your time to avoid causing any unintended damage. With the right approach and equipment, you can enjoy a beautifully cleaned home exterior that will be the envy of the neighborhood.

Concrete: Driveways, Sidewalks, and Patios

Concrete is one of the most durable and versatile building materials available, making it a popular choice for driveways, sidewalks, and patios. However, over time, concrete surfaces can become stained, discolored, and covered in dirt, grime, and other debris. Power washing is an effective way to restore the appearance of your concrete surfaces and keep them looking their best. In this chapter, we'll take a closer look at how to power wash concrete driveways, sidewalks, and patios.

Driveways

Concrete driveways are exposed to a lot of wear and tear from vehicles, foot traffic, and the elements. Over time, they can become stained with oil, grease, and other automotive fluids, as well as dirt, grime, and organic growth like moss and algae. Power washing is an effective way to remove these stains and restore the appearance of your driveway.

When power washing a concrete driveway, it's important to use a high-pressure setting and a narrow-angle nozzle to ensure maximum cleaning power. Start by removing any loose debris like leaves or twigs from the surface of the driveway. Then, apply a degreaser or concrete cleaner using a downstream injection method and let it sit for several minutes to penetrate any stubborn stains.

Use a high-pressure nozzle to blast away the dirt and grime, working in small sections and overlapping your strokes to ensure even coverage. Pay special attention to any oil or grease stains, as these may require additional treatment with a specialized cleaner.

Once you've finished power washing, rinse the driveway thoroughly with plain water to remove any remaining cleaning solution. If the driveway appears to be heavily stained or discolored, you may need to repeat the process or consider using a stronger cleaning solution.

Sidewalks

Concrete sidewalks are another common area that can benefit from power washing. Over time, sidewalks can become stained with dirt, grime, and organic growth like moss and algae, which can make them slippery and dangerous to walk on. Power washing can help to remove these stains and restore the appearance and safety of your sidewalks.

When power washing a concrete sidewalk, it's important to use a medium-pressure setting and a wide-angle nozzle to avoid damaging the surface. Start by removing any loose debris like leaves or twigs from the surface of the sidewalk. Then, apply a gentle cleaning solution using a downstream injection method and let it sit for a few minutes to penetrate any stubborn stains.

Use a medium-pressure nozzle to blast away the dirt and grime, working in small sections and overlapping your strokes to ensure even coverage. Pay special attention to any areas that are prone to organic growth, as these may require additional treatment with a specialized cleaner.

Once you've finished power washing, rinse the sidewalk thoroughly with plain water to remove any remaining cleaning solution. If the sidewalk appears to be heavily stained or discolored, you may need to repeat the process or consider using a stronger cleaning solution.

Patios

Concrete patios are a popular outdoor living space that can become stained and discolored over time due to exposure to the elements, foot traffic, and spills from outdoor cooking and entertaining. Power washing is an effective way to restore the appearance of your patio and keep it looking its best.

When power washing a concrete patio, it's important to use a medium-pressure setting and a wide-angle nozzle to avoid damaging the surface. Start by removing any furniture, potted plants, or other objects from the surface of the patio. Then, apply a gentle cleaning solution using a downstream injection method and let it sit for a few minutes to penetrate any stubborn stains.

Use a medium-pressure nozzle to blast away the dirt and grime, working in small sections and overlapping your strokes to ensure even coverage. Pay special attention to any areas that are prone to food or drink spills, as these may require additional treatment with a specialized cleaner.

Once you've finished power washing, rinse the patio thoroughly with plain water to remove any remaining cleaning solution. If the patio appears to be heavily stained or discolored, you may need to repeat the process or consider using a stronger cleaning solution.

By following these tips and techniques for power washing your concrete surfaces, you can keep them looking their best and extend their lifespan. Just remember to always prioritize safety and take your time to avoid causing any unintended damage. With the right approach and equipment, you can enjoy beautifully cleaned and maintained concrete surfaces that will enhance the overall appearance of your home.

Decks and Fences: Wood and Composite Materials

Decks and fences are popular outdoor structures that can add both functional and aesthetic value to your home. However, over time, these structures can become weathered, stained, and discolored due to exposure to the elements, foot traffic, and other factors. Power washing is an effective way to restore the appearance of your decks and fences and keep them looking their best. In this chapter, we'll take a closer look at how to power wash decks and fences made of wood and composite materials.

Wood Decks and Fences

Wood is a popular choice for decks and fences due to its natural beauty and durability. However, wood is also prone to weathering, staining, and decay if not properly maintained. Power washing is an effective way to remove dirt, grime, and other debris from the surface of your wood decks and fences, as well as prepare them for staining or sealing.

When power washing a wood deck or fence, it's important to use a low-pressure setting and a wide-angle nozzle to avoid damaging the wood fibers. Start by removing any furniture, potted plants, or other objects from the surface of the deck or fence. Then, apply a specialized wood cleaner using a downstream injection method and let it sit for several minutes to penetrate any stubborn stains.

Use a low-pressure nozzle to gently scrub the surface of the wood, working in small sections and following the grain of the wood to avoid damaging the fibers. Pay special attention to any areas that are prone to mold or mildew growth, as these may require additional treatment with a specialized cleaner.

Once you've finished power washing, rinse the deck or fence thoroughly with plain water to remove any remaining cleaning solution. Allow the wood to dry completely before applying any stain or sealer, as this will help to ensure even coverage and maximum protection.

Composite Decks and Fences

Composite decking and fencing materials are becoming increasingly popular due to their low maintenance requirements and durability. These materials are made from a combination of wood fibers and plastic polymers, which makes them resistant to weathering, staining, and decay. However, composite materials can still benefit from regular power washing to keep them looking their best.

When power washing a composite deck or fence, it's important to use a low-pressure setting and a wide-angle nozzle to avoid damaging the surface. Start by removing any furniture, potted plants, or other objects from the surface of the deck or fence. Then, apply a gentle cleaning solution using a downstream injection method and let it sit for a few minutes to penetrate any stubborn stains.

Use a low-pressure nozzle to gently scrub the surface of the composite material, working in small sections and overlapping your strokes to ensure even coverage. Pay special attention to any areas that are prone to mold or mildew growth, as these may require additional treatment with a specialized cleaner.

Once you've finished power washing, rinse the deck or fence thoroughly with plain water to remove any remaining cleaning solution. If the composite material appears to be heavily stained or discolored, you may need to repeat the process or consider using a stronger cleaning solution.

Tips for Power Washing Decks and Fences

Here are some additional tips to keep in mind when power washing your decks and fences:

1. Always test the pressure and nozzle settings on an inconspicuous area before beginning to ensure that you don't damage the surface.
2. Use a specialized cleaner that is appropriate for the type of material you are cleaning (e.g., wood, composite, etc.).
3. Work in small sections and overlap your strokes to ensure even coverage and avoid missed spots.
4. Rinse thoroughly with plain water to remove any remaining cleaning solution and prevent damage to the surface.
5. Allow the surface to dry completely before applying any stain, sealer, or other protective coating.

By following these tips and techniques for power washing your decks and fences, you can keep them looking their best and extend their lifespan. Just remember to always prioritize safety and take your time to avoid causing any unintended damage. With the right approach and equipment, you can enjoy beautifully cleaned and maintained outdoor structures that will enhance the overall appearance and value of your home.

Roofs: Asphalt Shingles and Tiles

The roof is one of the most critical components of your home, providing protection from the elements and helping to maintain the structural integrity of your house. However, over time, roofs can become dirty, stained, and covered in organic growth like moss and algae, which can lead to premature deterioration and decreased performance. Power washing is an effective way to clean and maintain your roof, but it's important to use the right techniques and equipment to avoid causing damage. In this chapter, we'll take a closer look at how to power wash roofs made of asphalt shingles and tiles.

Asphalt Shingle Roofs

Asphalt shingles are one of the most common roofing materials used in residential homes. They are affordable, durable, and relatively easy to maintain. However, asphalt shingles can still benefit from regular cleaning to remove dirt, debris, and organic growth that can lead to premature aging and decreased performance.

When power washing an asphalt shingle roof, it's important to use a low-pressure setting and a wide-angle nozzle to avoid damaging the shingles. Start by inspecting the roof for any loose or damaged shingles, and repair or replace them as necessary. Then, apply a specialized roof cleaner using a downstream injection method and let it sit for several minutes to penetrate any stubborn stains.

Use a low-pressure nozzle to gently scrub the surface of the shingles, working in small sections and following the natural water flow of the roof to avoid driving water underneath the shingles. Pay special attention to any areas that are prone to moss or algae growth, as these may require additional treatment with a specialized cleaner.

Once you've finished power washing, rinse the roof thoroughly with plain water to remove any remaining cleaning solution. Allow the roof to dry completely before inspecting it for any missed spots or areas that may require additional cleaning.

Tile Roofs

Tile roofs are another popular roofing material, particularly in warmer climates. They are durable, fire-resistant, and can last for many decades with proper maintenance. However, tile roofs can also become dirty and stained over time, and may require regular cleaning to keep them looking their best.

When power washing a tile roof, it's important to use a low-pressure setting and a wide-angle nozzle to avoid damaging the tiles. Start by inspecting the roof for any loose, cracked, or broken tiles, and repair or replace them as necessary. Then, apply a specialized tile cleaner using a downstream injection method and let it sit for several minutes to penetrate any stubborn stains.

Use a low-pressure nozzle to gently scrub the surface of the tiles, working in small sections and following the natural water flow of the roof to avoid driving water underneath the tiles. Pay special attention to any areas that are prone to moss or algae growth, as these may require additional treatment with a specialized cleaner.

Once you've finished power washing, rinse the roof thoroughly with plain water to remove any remaining cleaning solution. Allow the roof to dry completely before inspecting it for any missed spots or areas that may require additional cleaning.

Tips for Power Washing Roofs

Here are some additional tips to keep in mind when power washing your roof:

1. Always prioritize safety when working on your roof. Use proper safety equipment and techniques, and never work alone.
2. Use a specialized cleaner that is appropriate for the type of roofing material you are cleaning (e.g., asphalt shingles, tiles, etc.).
3. Work in small sections and follow the natural water flow of the roof to avoid driving water underneath the roofing material.
4. Rinse thoroughly with plain water to remove any remaining cleaning solution and prevent damage to the roof.
5. Allow the roof to dry completely before inspecting it for any missed spots or areas that may require additional cleaning.

By following these tips and techniques for power washing your roof, you can keep it looking its best and extend its lifespan. Just remember to always prioritize safety and take your time to avoid causing any unintended damage. With the right approach and equipment, you can enjoy a beautifully cleaned and maintained roof that will protect your home for years to come.

Masonry: Brick, Stone, and Stucco

Masonry is a popular building material that has been used for centuries in the construction of homes, buildings, and other structures. Brick, stone, and stucco are three of the most common types of masonry materials, each with its own unique characteristics and maintenance requirements. Over time, these materials can become dirty, stained, and covered in organic growth, which can detract from their appearance and lead to premature deterioration. Power washing is an effective way to clean and maintain masonry surfaces, but it's important to use the right techniques and equipment to avoid causing damage. In this chapter, we'll take a closer look at how to power wash brick, stone, and stucco surfaces.

Brick

Brick is a classic masonry material that is known for its durability, fire resistance, and aesthetic appeal. However, brick surfaces can become stained and discolored over time due to exposure to the elements, pollution, and other factors. Power washing is an effective way to remove dirt, grime, and stains from brick surfaces and restore their original color and texture.

When power washing brick, it's important to use a low-pressure setting and a wide-angle nozzle to avoid damaging the surface. Start by wetting down the surface with plain water to remove any loose dirt and debris. Then, apply a specialized brick cleaner using a downstream injection method and let it sit for several minutes to penetrate any stubborn stains.

Use a low-pressure nozzle to gently scrub the surface of the brick, working in small sections and following the natural pattern of the bricks to avoid damaging the mortar joints. Pay special attention to any areas that are prone to moss or algae growth, as these may require additional treatment with a specialized cleaner.

Once you've finished power washing, rinse the surface thoroughly with plain water to remove any remaining cleaning solution. Allow the brick to dry completely before inspecting it for any missed spots or areas that may require additional cleaning.

Stone

Stone is another popular masonry material that is prized for its natural beauty and durability. However, like brick, stone surfaces can become stained and discolored over time due to exposure to the elements and other factors. Power washing is an effective way to remove dirt, grime, and stains from stone surfaces and restore their original color and texture.

When power washing stone, it's important to use a low-pressure setting and a wide-angle nozzle to avoid damaging the surface. Start by wetting down the surface with plain water to remove any loose dirt and debris. Then, apply a specialized stone cleaner using a downstream injection method and let it sit for several minutes to penetrate any stubborn stains.

Use a low-pressure nozzle to gently scrub the surface of the stone, working in small sections and following the natural pattern of the stone to avoid damaging the surface. Pay special attention to any areas that are prone to moss or algae growth, as these may require additional treatment with a specialized cleaner.

Once you've finished power washing, rinse the surface thoroughly with plain water to remove any remaining cleaning solution. Allow the stone to dry completely before inspecting it for any missed spots or areas that may require additional cleaning.

Stucco

Stucco is a popular masonry material that is often used to cover the exterior walls of homes and buildings. It is known for its durability, fire resistance, and ability to provide insulation and soundproofing. However, like other masonry materials, stucco can become dirty and stained over time, and may require regular cleaning to maintain its appearance.

When power washing stucco, it's important to use a low-pressure setting and a wide-angle nozzle to avoid damaging the surface. Start by wetting down the surface with plain water to remove any loose dirt and debris. Then, apply a specialized stucco cleaner using a downstream injection method and let it sit for several minutes to penetrate any stubborn stains.

Use a low-pressure nozzle to gently scrub the surface of the stucco, working in small sections and using a circular motion to avoid damaging the surface. Pay special attention to any areas that are prone to mold or mildew growth, as these may require additional treatment with a specialized cleaner.

Once you've finished power washing, rinse the surface thoroughly with plain water to remove any remaining cleaning solution. Allow the stucco to dry completely before inspecting it for any missed spots or areas that may require additional cleaning.

Tips for Power Washing Masonry

Here are some additional tips to keep in mind when power washing masonry surfaces:

1. Always test the pressure and nozzle settings on an inconspicuous area before beginning to ensure that you don't damage the surface.

2. Use a specialized cleaner that is appropriate for the type of masonry material you are cleaning (e.g., brick, stone, stucco, etc.).
3. Work in small sections and use a gentle, circular motion to avoid damaging the surface.
4. Rinse thoroughly with plain water to remove any remaining cleaning solution and prevent damage to the surface.
5. Allow the surface to dry completely before applying any sealant or other protective coating.

By following these tips and techniques for power washing masonry surfaces, you can keep them looking their best and extend their lifespan. Just remember to always prioritize safety and take your time to avoid causing any unintended damage. With the right approach and equipment, you can enjoy beautifully cleaned and maintained masonry surfaces that will enhance the overall appearance and value of your home or building.

Chapter 3
Troubleshooting Common Power Washing Issues

Uneven Cleaning Results

Even with the best techniques and equipment, power washing can sometimes lead to unexpected issues or unsatisfactory results. One of the most common problems encountered during power washing is uneven cleaning results. In this section, we'll take a closer look at what causes uneven cleaning and how to troubleshoot and resolve this issue.

Uneven Cleaning Results

Uneven cleaning results can be frustrating and unsightly, leaving some areas of your surface clean while others remain dirty or stained. There are several factors that can contribute to uneven cleaning, including:

1. Inconsistent pressure: If the pressure of your power washer is not consistent throughout the cleaning process, it can lead to uneven results. This can happen if the pressure drops due to a leak in the hose or a clogged nozzle.

2. Incorrect nozzle: Using the wrong nozzle for your surface or cleaning task can also lead to uneven results. For example, using a narrow-angle nozzle on a delicate surface can cause damage and leave streaks or lines.

3. Improper technique: If you are not using the correct technique for your surface or cleaning task, it can lead to uneven results. For example, if you are not overlapping your strokes or if you are holding the nozzle too close or too far away from the surface.

4. Dirty or clogged equipment: If your power washer or nozzle is dirty or clogged, it can affect the spray pattern and lead to uneven cleaning results.

To troubleshoot and resolve uneven cleaning results, try the following steps:

1. Check your pressure: Make sure that your power washer is delivering consistent pressure throughout the cleaning process. If you notice a drop in pressure, check for leaks in the hose or clogs in the nozzle.

2. Use the right nozzle: Make sure that you are using the appropriate nozzle for your surface and cleaning task. Refer to your power washer's manual or the manufacturer's recommendations for guidance.

3. Adjust your technique: Make sure that you are using the correct technique for your surface and cleaning task. Overlap your strokes, keep the nozzle at the appropriate distance from the surface, and use a consistent speed and pattern.

4. Clean your equipment: If your power washer or nozzle is dirty or clogged, clean it thoroughly before continuing with your cleaning task. Follow the manufacturer's instructions for cleaning and maintenance.

5. Test on an inconspicuous area: Before cleaning the entire surface, test your power washer on a small, inconspicuous area to make sure that you are using the right pressure, nozzle, and technique for your specific surface.

In addition to these troubleshooting steps, there are a few other tips to keep in mind to prevent uneven cleaning results:

1. Work in small sections: Rather than trying to clean the entire surface at once, work in small sections and complete each section before moving on to the next. This will help ensure that you are applying even pressure and technique throughout the entire surface.

2. Use a cleaner: If you are having trouble removing stubborn stains or debris, consider using a specialized cleaner designed for your specific surface. Follow the manufacturer's instructions for application and removal.

3. Rinse thoroughly: After cleaning, make sure to rinse the surface thoroughly with plain water to remove any remaining cleaning solution and debris. This will help prevent streaks or residue from forming on the surface.

By following these troubleshooting steps and tips, you can resolve uneven cleaning results and achieve a consistently clean and beautiful surface. Remember to always prioritize safety and take your time to avoid causing any unintended damage. With the right approach and equipment, you can enjoy the many benefits of power washing and maintain the appearance and integrity of your surfaces for years to come.

Damage to Surfaces

One of the most significant concerns when power washing is the potential for damage to the surfaces being cleaned. While power washing can be an effective way to remove dirt, grime, and stains, it can also cause harm to delicate or sensitive surfaces if not done correctly. In this section, we'll explore the various types of surface damage that can occur during power washing and how to prevent and address them.

Types of Surface Damage

1. Etching: Etching occurs when the high-pressure water stream from the power washer creates small, shallow grooves or lines in the surface being cleaned. This is most common on softer surfaces like wood or certain types of stone.

2. Gouging: Gouging is a more severe form of etching, where the water pressure is high enough to create deep, visible scars in the surface. This can be caused by using too high of a pressure setting, holding the nozzle too close to the surface, or using the wrong nozzle for the job.

3. Stripping: Stripping happens when the power washer removes not just the dirt and grime, but also the top layer of the surface itself. This can be a particular problem with painted or stained surfaces, where the finish can be blasted away by the high-pressure water.

4. Pitting: Pitting refers to the formation of small, shallow holes in the surface being cleaned. This is most common on softer, more porous surfaces like certain types of brick or concrete.

5. Scarring: Scarring is a general term for any visible damage or marring of the surface caused by the power washer. This can include etching, gouging, stripping, or pitting, as well as other types of marks or blemishes.

Preventing Surface Damage

The best way to deal with surface damage is to prevent it from happening in the first place. Here are some tips to help minimize the risk of damage when power washing:

1. Use the right pressure setting: Always start with the lowest pressure setting that will still effectively clean the surface, and only increase the pressure if necessary. Using too high of a pressure setting is one of the most common causes of surface damage.

2. Choose the right nozzle: Different nozzles are designed for different cleaning tasks and surfaces. Using the wrong nozzle can lead to surface damage, so be sure to consult your power washer's manual or the manufacturer's recommendations.

3. Keep the nozzle at the proper distance: Holding the nozzle too close to the surface can cause etching, gouging, or other types of damage. As a general rule, keep the nozzle about 12-18 inches away from the surface being cleaned.

4. Use a gentler technique: When power washing, use a sweeping motion and avoid focusing the spray on one spot for too long. This will help distribute the water pressure evenly and reduce the risk of damage.

5. Test on an inconspicuous area: Before cleaning the entire surface, test your power washer on a small, inconspicuous area to make sure that you are using the right pressure, nozzle, and technique for your specific surface.

Addressing Surface Damage

If surface damage does occur during power washing, there are a few steps you can take to address it:

1. Stop power washing immediately: If you notice any signs of surface damage, stop power washing right away to prevent further harm.

2. Assess the damage: Carefully examine the affected area to determine the type and extent of the damage. This will help you decide on the best course of action.

3. Make repairs as needed: Depending on the type and severity of the damage, you may need to make repairs to the surface. This could involve filling in etched or gouged areas, sanding down rough spots, or even replacing damaged sections altogether.

4. Consider professional help: If the damage is extensive or if you are unsure how to properly repair it, consider hiring a professional contractor who specializes in surface restoration.

By taking these steps and following the tips for preventing surface damage, you can minimize the risk of harm to your surfaces during power washing. Remember to always prioritize safety and take your time to ensure the best possible results. With the right approach and equipment, you can enjoy the many benefits of power washing without compromising the integrity of your surfaces.

Clogged or Malfunctioning Equipment

Power washing equipment is designed to deliver high-pressure water to effectively clean various surfaces. However, like any mechanical device, power washers can experience issues such as clogging or malfunctioning. These problems can lead to reduced cleaning efficiency, uneven results, or even complete equipment failure. In this section, we'll discuss the common causes of clogged or malfunctioning power washing equipment and how to troubleshoot and resolve these issues.

Causes of Clogged or Malfunctioning Equipment

1. Dirty or contaminated water supply: If the water supply used for power washing contains dirt, debris, or other contaminants, it can clog the nozzle, hose, or pump over time.

2. Improper nozzle usage: Using the wrong nozzle for a specific task or allowing the nozzle to become worn or damaged can result in clogs or malfunctions.

3. Insufficient water pressure: If the water pressure supplied to the power washer is too low, it can lead to poor performance and potential clogs.

4. Damaged or worn components: Over time, various power washer components, such as O-rings, seals, or valves, can become worn or damaged, causing leaks or malfunctions.

5. Lack of maintenance: Failing to perform regular maintenance tasks, such as cleaning the nozzle, inspecting the hose, or replacing the oil, can result in clogs or malfunctions.

Troubleshooting Clogged or Malfunctioning Equipment

1. Check the water supply: Ensure that the water source is clean and free of contaminants. If necessary, use a water filter to remove any dirt or debris.

2. Inspect the nozzle: Check the nozzle for any signs of wear, damage, or clogs. Clean the nozzle thoroughly with a nozzle cleaning tool or replace it if needed.

3. Verify water pressure: Make sure that the water pressure supplied to the power washer meets the manufacturer's specifications. Low water pressure can be caused by a variety of factors, such as a partially closed valve or a leak in the supply line.

4. Examine the hose: Inspect the hose for any kinks, cuts, or leaks. A damaged hose can restrict water flow and cause clogs or malfunctions.

5. Check for leaks: Look for any signs of water leaks around the pump, hose connections, or spray gun. Leaks can indicate worn or damaged components that may need to be replaced.

6. Perform regular maintenance: Follow the manufacturer's recommended maintenance schedule, which may include tasks such as changing the oil, replacing the spark plug, or cleaning the air filter.

Resolving Clogged or Malfunctioning Equipment

1. Clean or replace the nozzle: If the nozzle is clogged, use a nozzle cleaning tool to remove any debris. If the nozzle is damaged or worn, replace it with a new one.

2. Flush the system: Run clean water through the power washer for several minutes to flush out any dirt or debris that may be causing clogs.

3. Repair or replace damaged components: If you identify any damaged or worn components, such as O-rings, seals, or valves, repair or replace them as needed.

4. Adjust the water pressure: If the water pressure is too low, check for any partially closed valves or leaks in the supply line. Adjust the pressure regulator on the power washer if needed.

5. Contact the manufacturer or a professional: If you are unable to resolve the issue on your own, contact the manufacturer's customer support or a professional power washing service for assistance.

Prevention and Maintenance

To minimize the risk of clogged or malfunctioning power washing equipment, follow these prevention and maintenance tips:

1. Use clean water: Always use a clean, debris-free water source for power washing. Consider using a water filter if necessary.

2. Select the appropriate nozzle: Choose the right nozzle for each specific task and surface to avoid damage or clogs.

3. Handle equipment with care: Be gentle when handling the hose, spray gun, and other components to prevent damage or leaks.

4. Store properly: After each use, drain the water from the power washer, and store it in a dry, protected area to prevent rust or damage.

5. Perform regular maintenance: Follow the manufacturer's recommended maintenance schedule to keep your power washer in optimal condition.

By understanding the causes of clogged or malfunctioning power washing equipment and following these troubleshooting, resolution, and maintenance tips, you can ensure that your power washer operates efficiently and effectively. Regular maintenance and proper usage will not only extend the life of your equipment but also help you achieve the best possible cleaning results.

Persistent Stains and Grime

Despite the power and effectiveness of pressure washing, some stains and grime can be particularly stubborn and challenging to remove. These persistent stains may require additional techniques, cleaning solutions, or even multiple cleaning sessions to achieve the desired results. In this section, we'll explore the common types of persistent stains and grime encountered during power washing and provide strategies for tackling these tough cleaning challenges.

Common Types of Persistent Stains and Grime

1. Oil and grease stains: Driveways, garage floors, and other concrete surfaces can develop tough oil and grease stains from vehicles, machinery, or cooking equipment.

2. Rust stains: Metal furniture, tools, or other objects can leave rust stains on various surfaces, particularly concrete or stone.

3. Paint stains: Drips, spills, or overspray from painting projects can create stubborn stains on a variety of surfaces.

4. Mold and mildew: In damp, shaded areas, mold and mildew can grow on surfaces like wood, concrete, or siding, leading to discoloration and potential health hazards.

5. Chewing gum: Chewing gum can adhere strongly to concrete, asphalt, or other surfaces, making it difficult to remove.

6. Hard water stains: In areas with high mineral content in the water supply, hard water stains can build up on surfaces like glass, tile, or metal.

Strategies for Removing Persistent Stains and Grime

1. Pre-treat the stain: Before power washing, apply a specialized cleaning solution or stain remover directly to the affected area. Allow the solution to penetrate the stain for the recommended time before proceeding with power washing.

2. Use a higher pressure setting: If the stain persists after initial cleaning, try increasing the pressure setting on your power washer. Be cautious, as higher pressure can potentially damage some surfaces.

3. Employ a hot water power washer: Some professional-grade power washers can heat the water, which can be more effective in breaking down tough stains and grime.

4. Utilize a surface cleaner attachment: A surface cleaner attachment for your power washer can help distribute the water pressure evenly and provide a more thorough clean for flat surfaces like driveways or patios.

5. Repeat the cleaning process: For particularly stubborn stains, it may be necessary to repeat the cleaning process multiple times. Be patient and persistent, as some stains may require several passes to fully remove.

6. Scrub with a brush: In some cases, scrubbing the stain with a stiff-bristled brush before or during power washing can help loosen the grime and make it easier to remove.

7. Consult a professional: If the stain remains after exhausting these strategies, it may be time to consult a professional power washing service. They may have access to more advanced equipment, cleaning solutions, or techniques to address the issue.

Prevention and Maintenance

To minimize the occurrence of persistent stains and grime, consider the following prevention and maintenance tips:

1. Clean spills immediately: When spills occur, clean them up as quickly as possible to prevent them from setting into the surface and becoming harder to remove.

2. Perform regular cleaning: Establish a regular cleaning schedule for your surfaces to prevent the buildup of dirt, grime, and stains over time.

3. Apply protective coatings: Use sealers, waxes, or other protective coatings on surfaces like concrete, stone, or wood to create a barrier against stains and make cleaning easier.

4. Address moisture issues: To prevent mold and mildew growth, ensure that surfaces are properly sealed and that areas with high moisture or limited sunlight have adequate ventilation.

5. Avoid harsh chemicals: When cleaning, opt for environmentally-friendly, non-toxic cleaning solutions to prevent potential damage to your surfaces or the surrounding landscape.

By understanding the common types of persistent stains and grime and employing these removal strategies and prevention tips, you can effectively tackle even the toughest cleaning challenges. Remember to always test a small, inconspicuous area before applying any new cleaning solution or technique, and prioritize safety when using power washing equipment. With patience, persistence, and the right approach, you can restore your surfaces to their original beauty and maintain them for years to come.

Chapter 4
Maintenance and Storage
Cleaning and Storing Your Power Washer

Proper maintenance and storage of your power washing equipment are essential for ensuring its longevity, reliability, and optimal performance. Regular maintenance tasks and correct storage procedures can help prevent malfunctions, prolong the life of your equipment, and make your power washing experience more efficient and effective. In this section, we'll focus on the importance of cleaning and storing your power washer and provide a detailed guide on how to do so.

Cleaning and Storing Your Power Washer

Cleaning your power washer after each use is crucial for preventing the buildup of dirt, grime, and mineral deposits that can clog or damage the components. Proper storage is equally important to protect your equipment from environmental factors that can cause rust, corrosion, or other damage. Follow these steps to clean and store your power washer correctly:

1. Disconnect the power supply: Before cleaning your power washer, ensure that it is turned off and disconnected from the power source, whether it's an electrical outlet or a gas tank.

2. Drain the water: Remove any remaining water from the hose, spray gun, and nozzle by running the power washer for a few seconds without the water supply connected. This will help prevent freezing and damage to the components in cold storage conditions.

3. Clean the nozzle: Remove the nozzle from the spray gun and clean it thoroughly with a nozzle cleaning tool or a soft-bristled brush. Ensure that any dirt or debris is removed from the nozzle openings to prevent clogs during the next use.

4. Wipe down the exterior: Use a clean, damp cloth to wipe down the exterior of the power washer, including the hose, spray gun, and wand. Remove any dirt, grime, or debris that may have accumulated during use.

5. Lubricate O-rings: Apply a small amount of O-ring lubricant to the O-rings on the spray gun and wand to keep them pliable and prevent leaks.

6. Drain the pump: If your power washer has a detergent injection system, run clean water through the system for a few minutes to flush out any remaining detergent. Then, locate the pump drain plug (consult your owner's manual if necessary) and remove it to allow any remaining water to drain from the pump.

7. Store in a dry, protected area: Once your power washer is clean and dry, store it in a dry, protected area away from direct sunlight, rain, or freezing temperatures. If possible, store the power washer indoors, such as in a garage or shed.

8. Cover the power washer: Use a breathable cover or tarp to protect your power washer from dust, dirt, and debris while in storage.

9. Perform off-season maintenance: If you plan to store your power washer for an extended period, such as during the winter months, perform additional maintenance tasks as recommended by the manufacturer. This may include adding fuel stabilizer to the gas tank, changing the oil, or removing the spark plug.

By following these cleaning and storage steps, you can ensure that your power washer remains in excellent condition and is ready to use when needed. Regular maintenance will not only extend the life of your equipment but also improve its performance and reliability.

Additional Maintenance Tips

In addition to cleaning and storing your power washer properly, consider these maintenance tips to keep your equipment in top shape:

1. Inspect the hose and connections: Regularly check the hose and connections for any signs of wear, damage, or leaks. Replace any damaged components promptly to prevent further damage or malfunctions.

2. Check the oil level: If your power washer has a gas engine, check the oil level before each use and change the oil according to the manufacturer's recommendations.

3. Clean or replace the air filter: A clean air filter ensures that your power washer's engine receives an adequate air supply. Clean or replace the air filter as needed, following the manufacturer's guidelines.

4. Tighten bolts and screws: Periodically check and tighten any loose bolts, screws, or other fasteners to prevent vibration and damage to your power washer.

5. Schedule professional servicing: Consider having your power washer professionally serviced every year or as recommended by the manufacturer. A professional technician can identify and address any potential issues before they become more serious problems.

By incorporating these maintenance and storage practices into your power washing routine, you can maximize the performance, efficiency, and lifespan of your equipment. Proper care and storage will not only save you time and money in the long run but also ensure that your power washer is always ready to tackle any cleaning challenge that comes its way.

Maintaining Exterior Surfaces Between Washes

While power washing is an effective way to thoroughly clean and refresh your home's exterior surfaces, it's equally important to maintain these surfaces between washes to keep them looking their best and to prevent the buildup of dirt, grime, and stains. Regular maintenance can also help extend the time between power washing sessions, saving you time and effort in the long run. In this section, we'll discuss various strategies for maintaining your exterior surfaces between power washes.

1. Regularly sweep and rinse surfaces

One of the simplest and most effective ways to maintain your exterior surfaces between power washes is to regularly sweep and rinse them with a garden hose. This is particularly important for surfaces like driveways, patios, and decks, which can accumulate dirt, leaves, and other debris over time. By removing this debris before it has a chance to settle into the surface or stain it, you can keep your surfaces looking cleaner for longer.

2. Spot clean stains promptly

When spills or stains occur on your exterior surfaces, it's essential to address them as quickly as possible to prevent them from setting in and becoming more difficult to remove. Keep a supply of appropriate cleaning solutions on hand, such as a degreaser for oil stains on a driveway or a mild detergent for food or drink spills on a deck. Apply the cleaning solution to the affected area, scrub gently with a soft-bristled brush, and rinse thoroughly with water.

3. Trim nearby vegetation

Overhanging trees, shrubs, and other vegetation can contribute to the buildup of dirt, debris, and organic matter on your exterior surfaces.

Regularly trimming back this vegetation can help reduce the amount of debris that accumulates on your surfaces and can also improve air circulation and sunlight exposure, which can help prevent the growth of mold and mildew.

4. Clean gutters and downspouts

Clogged gutters and downspouts can cause water to overflow and spill onto your exterior surfaces, leading to staining, erosion, and even foundation damage. Regularly cleaning your gutters and downspouts, particularly in the fall and spring, can help ensure that water is properly channeled away from your home and its exterior surfaces.

5. Apply protective coatings

Applying protective coatings to your exterior surfaces can help repel dirt, stains, and moisture, making them easier to maintain between power washes. For example, applying a sealant to a concrete driveway can help prevent oil and other stains from penetrating the surface, while applying a stain or sealant to a wooden deck can help protect it from water damage and UV rays.

6. Address any repairs promptly

Promptly addressing any necessary repairs to your exterior surfaces can help prevent further damage and make maintenance easier in the long run. For example, filling cracks in a concrete driveway can help prevent water from seeping in and causing further damage, while replacing loose or damaged boards on a deck can help ensure a safe and attractive surface.

7. Maintain a regular cleaning schedule

Establishing and sticking to a regular cleaning schedule for your exterior surfaces can help keep them looking their best and can make power washing sessions more manageable. Consider creating a calendar or checklist of monthly, quarterly, and annual maintenance tasks, such as sweeping, rinsing, and applying protective coatings.

By implementing these maintenance strategies between power washes, you can help extend the life and beauty of your home's exterior surfaces. Regular maintenance not only keeps your surfaces looking cleaner and more attractive but can also save you time, effort, and money in the long run by preventing the buildup of stubborn stains and grime that can be more difficult to remove.

Remember, the key to successful exterior surface maintenance is consistency and promptness. By staying on top of regular cleaning and maintenance tasks and addressing any issues as soon as they arise, you can enjoy a beautiful, well-maintained home exterior that you can be proud of. When the time does come for a full power wash, you'll find that the process is quicker, easier, and more effective thanks to your ongoing maintenance efforts.

Scheduling Regular Power Washing Sessions

Incorporating regular power washing sessions into your home maintenance routine is essential for keeping your exterior surfaces clean, attractive, and in good condition. However, knowing how often to power wash and when to schedule these sessions can be a challenge. In this section, we'll discuss the factors to consider when scheduling regular power washing sessions and provide guidance on creating an effective power washing schedule.

Factors to Consider

1. Surface type and material

The type of surface and material you're cleaning will play a significant role in determining how often you should power wash. Some surfaces, like vinyl siding or glass, may only require annual cleaning, while others, like wooden decks or concrete driveways, may benefit from more frequent washing to prevent the buildup of dirt, grime, and stains.

2. Environmental factors

The environment in which your home is located can also impact how often you need to power wash. Homes in areas with high humidity, frequent rainfall, or dense vegetation may require more frequent cleaning to prevent the growth of mold, mildew, and algae. Similarly, homes in areas with high levels of air pollution or near construction sites may accumulate dirt and grime more quickly and require more frequent washing.

3. Usage and traffic

The amount of usage and foot traffic your exterior surfaces receive can also affect how often they need to be power washed. Surfaces that see a lot of activity, like a busy driveway or a frequently used deck, may require more frequent cleaning to remove accumulated dirt and stains.

4. Personal preference and aesthetic goals

Ultimately, the frequency of your power washing sessions will also depend on your personal preferences and aesthetic goals. If you prefer a consistently clean and pristine appearance for your home's exterior, you may choose to power wash more frequently than someone who is content with a more lived-in look.

Creating a Power Washing Schedule

Based on the factors discussed above, here are some general guidelines for scheduling regular power washing sessions:

1. Annual washing

At a minimum, aim to power wash your home's exterior surfaces at least once a year. This annual washing can help remove accumulated dirt, grime, and stains and can help prevent the buildup of more stubborn debris over time.

2. Spring and fall washing

For surfaces that require more frequent cleaning, like wooden decks or concrete driveways, consider scheduling power washing sessions in the spring and fall. Spring washing can help remove any dirt and debris that accumulated over the winter, while fall washing can help prepare your surfaces for the harsher weather ahead.

3. Quarterly washing

In some cases, such as homes in particularly humid or polluted environments, quarterly power washing may be necessary to keep exterior surfaces clean and in good condition. This is also a good option for surfaces that see a lot of usage and traffic.

4. Monthly maintenance

While monthly power washing is generally not necessary, incorporating regular maintenance tasks like sweeping, rinsing, and spot cleaning into your monthly routine can help keep your exterior surfaces looking their best between more thorough power washing sessions.

When creating your power washing schedule, be sure to consider your own unique circumstances and goals. If you're unsure how often to power wash a particular surface, consult with a professional power washing company for guidance.

Tips for Successful Power Washing Sessions

To ensure that your regular power washing sessions are as effective and efficient as possible, keep these tips in mind:

1. Choose the right time of day

Aim to power wash during the cooler parts of the day, like early morning or late afternoon, to avoid the surface drying too quickly and leaving behind streaks or spots.

2. Prepare the area

Before beginning your power washing session, take the time to prepare the area by removing any obstacles, covering plants or landscaping, and protecting any electrical outlets or fixtures.

3. Use the right equipment and techniques

Be sure to use the appropriate power washer settings, nozzles, and cleaning solutions for the surface you're cleaning, and follow proper techniques to avoid damaging the surface or leaving behind streaks or uneven cleaning.

4. Rinse thoroughly

After power washing, be sure to rinse the surface thoroughly with clean water to remove any remaining cleaning solution or debris.

5. Allow adequate drying time
Give your surfaces plenty of time to dry completely before walking on them or replacing any furniture or decorations.

By scheduling regular power washing sessions and following these tips, you can keep your home's exterior surfaces looking their best and can extend their lifespan by preventing the buildup of damaging dirt, grime, and stains. Remember, a little bit of regular maintenance can go a long way in preserving the beauty and value of your home.

Chapter 4
Eco-Friendly Power Washing Practices

Using Biodegradable Cleaning Solutions

As concerns about environmental sustainability continue to grow, it's becoming increasingly important to consider the impact of our home maintenance practices, including power washing. By adopting eco-friendly power washing practices, we can minimize our environmental footprint while still effectively cleaning and maintaining our home's exterior surfaces. In this section, we'll focus on one key aspect of eco-friendly power washing: using biodegradable cleaning solutions.

Using Biodegradable Cleaning Solutions

One of the most significant ways to make your power washing practices more environmentally friendly is to choose biodegradable cleaning solutions over traditional chemical-based options. Biodegradable cleaning solutions are designed to break down naturally in the environment without leaving behind harmful residues or pollutants.

Benefits of Biodegradable Cleaning Solutions

1. Reduced environmental impact

Biodegradable cleaning solutions are less harmful to the environment than traditional chemical-based options. As they break down, they don't release toxic substances into the soil, water, or air, which helps to preserve the health and balance of local ecosystems.

2. Safer for plants and animals

Because biodegradable cleaning solutions don't leave behind harmful residues, they are safer for plants, animals, and other living organisms that may come into contact with the cleaned surfaces or the runoff from the power washing process.

3. Gentler on surfaces

Many biodegradable cleaning solutions are also gentler on the surfaces being cleaned, which can help to prevent damage or deterioration over time. This is particularly important for delicate surfaces like wood or soft stone.

4. Better for human health

By reducing exposure to harsh chemicals, biodegradable cleaning solutions are also better for human health. This is especially important for those with allergies, sensitivities, or respiratory issues who may be more affected by exposure to chemical fumes or residues.

Choosing Biodegradable Cleaning Solutions

When selecting biodegradable cleaning solutions for your power washing needs, look for products that are:

1. Certified biodegradable

Look for cleaning solutions that are certified biodegradable by reputable organizations like the Environmental Protection Agency (EPA) or the United States Department of Agriculture (USDA).

2. Plant-based or natural ingredients

Prefer cleaning solutions that are made from plant-based or natural ingredients, as these are more likely to be biodegradable and environmentally friendly.

3. Free from harmful chemicals

Avoid cleaning solutions that contain harmful chemicals like bleach, ammonia, or phosphates, as these can be toxic to the environment and living organisms.

4. Concentrated formulas

Choose concentrated formulas that can be diluted with water, as this reduces packaging waste and makes the products more economical and environmentally friendly.

Tips for Using Biodegradable Cleaning Solutions

To get the most out of your biodegradable cleaning solutions and to ensure the best results for your power washing projects, follow these tips:

1. Read and follow instructions carefully

Be sure to read and follow the manufacturer's instructions for dilution, application, and rinsing to ensure the best results and to avoid any potential damage to surfaces or the environment.

2. Test on a small area first

Before using a new biodegradable cleaning solution on a large surface, test it on a small, inconspicuous area first to ensure that it won't cause any discoloration or damage.

3. Allow adequate soaking time

Many biodegradable cleaning solutions work best when allowed to soak into the surface for a period of time before rinsing. Follow the manufacturer's recommendations for soaking time to achieve optimal results.

4. Rinse thoroughly

After cleaning with a biodegradable solution, be sure to rinse the surface thoroughly with clean water to remove any remaining residue and to prevent any potential harm to plants or animals that may come into contact with the surface.

By choosing and using biodegradable cleaning solutions for your power washing needs, you can take a significant step towards more eco-friendly and sustainable home maintenance practices. Not only will you be minimizing your environmental impact, but you'll also be creating a safer, healthier environment for yourself, your family, and your community.

Remember, small changes can add up to a big difference over time. By making a conscious effort to adopt more eco-friendly power washing practices, you'll be contributing to a cleaner, greener future for generations to come.

Conserving Water During Power Washing

Water conservation is an essential aspect of eco-friendly power washing practices. By taking steps to minimize water usage during the power washing process, we can reduce our environmental impact, lower our utility bills, and help to preserve one of our most precious natural resources. In this section, we'll explore several strategies for conserving water during power washing.

1. Use a high-efficiency nozzle

One of the most effective ways to conserve water during power washing is to use a high-efficiency nozzle. These nozzles are designed to deliver a more concentrated and powerful stream of water, which allows you to clean surfaces more effectively while using less water overall. Look for nozzles with a 15-degree or 25-degree spray pattern, as these tend to be the most efficient.

2. Adjust pressure settings

Another way to conserve water during power washing is to adjust the pressure settings on your power washer. Using a higher pressure setting than necessary can waste water and potentially damage surfaces. Instead, start with a lower pressure setting and gradually increase it until you find the minimum pressure needed to effectively clean the surface.

3. Use a pressure washer with an adjustable flow rate

Some pressure washers come with an adjustable flow rate feature, which allows you to control the amount of water being used. By reducing the flow rate, you can conserve water without sacrificing cleaning power. Look for a pressure washer with this feature when making a new purchase, or consider upgrading your existing equipment.

4. Incorporate a surface cleaner attachment

A surface cleaner attachment is a specialized tool that connects to your pressure washer wand and uses a rotating brush to clean flat surfaces like driveways, sidewalks, and patios. These attachments are designed to clean more efficiently than a standard nozzle, which means they can help you conserve water while still achieving excellent results.

5. Use a water broom attachment

Similar to a surface cleaner attachment, a water broom attachment is designed to clean large, flat surfaces more efficiently than a standard nozzle. Water broom attachments feature a wide, flat spray pattern that covers more surface area with each pass, helping you to conserve water and reduce cleaning time.

6. Collect and reuse rinse water

When power washing, a significant amount of water is used for rinsing surfaces after cleaning. To conserve water, consider collecting the rinse water in a bucket or basin and reusing it for other purposes, such as watering plants or washing your car. Just be sure to use caution when reusing water that may contain cleaning solution residue, as this can be harmful to some plants and surfaces.

7. Fix leaks and maintain equipment

Leaks in your power washing equipment can waste a significant amount of water over time. Regularly inspect your hoses, nozzles, and connections for leaks, and promptly repair or replace any damaged components. Proper maintenance of your power washing equipment can also help to ensure that it is operating at peak efficiency, which can help to conserve water and energy.

Tips for Conserving Water

In addition to the strategies outlined above, there are several general tips you can follow to conserve water during power washing:

1. Plan your cleaning strategically

Before beginning a power washing project, take the time to plan your cleaning approach strategically. Identify the areas that need the most attention and focus your efforts there, rather than wasting water on areas that may not require as much cleaning.

2. Avoid cleaning on windy days

Cleaning on windy days can result in wasted water, as wind can carry spray and mist away from the intended surface. Wait for a calm day to power wash for optimal water conservation.

3. Turn off the water when not in use

When moving between surfaces or taking breaks, be sure to turn off the water supply to your power washer to avoid wasting water.

4. Use a low-flow hose nozzle

When rinsing surfaces after power washing, consider using a low-flow hose nozzle to reduce water usage. These nozzles are designed to deliver a smaller volume of water while still providing adequate rinsing power.

By implementing these water conservation strategies and tips, you can significantly reduce your water usage during power washing without sacrificing the quality of your results. Not only will you be doing your part to protect the environment, but you'll also be saving money on your water bills and helping to ensure a more sustainable future for us all.

Remember, every drop counts when it comes to water conservation. By making a conscious effort to use water more efficiently and responsibly during power washing, you'll be setting a positive example for others and contributing to a greener, more sustainable world.

Proper Disposal of Wastewater and Debris

When power washing, it's essential to consider the proper disposal of wastewater and debris to minimize environmental impact and comply with local regulations. Wastewater from power washing can contain a variety of contaminants, such as dirt, grime, cleaning solutions, and pollutants, which can harm the environment if not disposed of properly. Similarly, debris removed during the power washing process must be handled and disposed of responsibly to prevent pollution and protect local ecosystems. In this section, we'll discuss best practices for the proper disposal of wastewater and debris generated during power washing.

Wastewater Disposal

1. Follow local regulations

Before disposing of power washing wastewater, familiarize yourself with local regulations and guidelines. Many municipalities have specific requirements for the disposal of wastewater containing cleaning solutions or other contaminants. Contact your local water authority or environmental agency for guidance on proper disposal methods in your area.

2. Use a containment system

To prevent wastewater from entering storm drains, waterways, or soil, use a containment system to collect and contain the water during the power washing process. This can be as simple as using a large tarp or plastic sheet to direct the wastewater towards a central collection point, such as a sump pump or wet/dry vacuum.

3. Filter the wastewater

Before disposing of the collected wastewater, it's important to remove any debris or contaminants. Use a fine mesh screen or filter to remove solid particles, and consider using a water treatment product to neutralize any remaining cleaning solutions or pollutants.

4. Dispose of wastewater properly

Once the wastewater has been collected and filtered, dispose of it according to local regulations. In many cases, this may involve directing the water into a sanitary sewer system, such as a toilet or utility sink. Avoid disposing of wastewater in storm drains, as these typically lead directly to local waterways without treatment.

Debris Disposal

1. Collect debris thoroughly

During the power washing process, debris such as dirt, grime, and organic matter will be removed from the surface being cleaned. Use a broom, rake, or wet/dry vacuum to collect this debris thoroughly, ensuring that no particles are left behind to be washed into storm drains or waterways.

2. Separate hazardous materials

If the debris contains any hazardous materials, such as oil, paint, or chemicals, these must be separated from the general debris and disposed of according to local regulations for hazardous waste. Contact your local waste management authority for guidance on proper disposal methods for these materials.

3. Dispose of organic matter responsibly

Organic matter, such as leaves, twigs, and grass clippings, can be disposed of in a compost bin or used as mulch in your garden. Avoid disposing of organic matter in plastic bags, as this can contribute to landfill waste and prevent the materials from decomposing naturally.

4. Recycle or dispose of solid waste

Any remaining solid waste, such as plastic, paper, or metal debris, should be sorted and recycled or disposed of according to local guidelines. Many municipalities have specific requirements for the disposal of construction or demolition waste, so be sure to follow these regulations when disposing of debris from power washing projects.

Tips for Minimizing Waste

To reduce the amount of wastewater and debris generated during power washing, consider the following tips:

1. Use eco-friendly cleaning solutions

Choose biodegradable, non-toxic cleaning solutions to minimize the environmental impact of your power washing wastewater.

2. Employ preventive measures

Regularly sweep and maintain surfaces to prevent the buildup of dirt and debris, reducing the amount of waste generated during power washing.

3. Use a lower pressure setting

When possible, use a lower pressure setting on your power washer to minimize the amount of debris and wastewater generated.

4. Reuse wastewater when appropriate

If the wastewater from your power washing project is free from harmful contaminants, consider reusing it for irrigation or other non-potable purposes to conserve water.

By following these best practices for the proper disposal of wastewater and debris, you can ensure that your power washing projects are environmentally responsible and compliant with local regulations. Remember, the goal is to minimize our impact on the environment while still achieving effective cleaning results.

In addition to proper disposal, it's important to educate ourselves and others about the importance of responsible power washing practices. By sharing our knowledge and setting a positive example, we can encourage more people to adopt eco-friendly and sustainable cleaning methods, ultimately contributing to a cleaner, healthier environment for generations to come.

Chapter 6
Advanced Power Washing Applications

Graffiti Removal

As you become more experienced and proficient with power washing, you may encounter more challenging cleaning projects that require advanced techniques and specialized knowledge. One such application is graffiti removal, which can be a difficult and time-consuming task. In this section, we'll explore the process of removing graffiti using power washing and provide tips for achieving the best results.

Graffiti Removal

Graffiti is a form of vandalism that involves the unauthorized application of paint, markers, or other substances to public or private property. Not only is graffiti unsightly, but it can also contribute to a sense of disorder and neglect in a community. Prompt removal of graffiti is essential for maintaining a clean and welcoming environment, and power washing can be an effective tool for this purpose.

Assessing the Surface and Graffiti

Before attempting to remove graffiti with a power washer, it's important to assess both the surface and the graffiti itself. Different types of surfaces, such as brick, concrete, or metal, may require different cleaning approaches and pressure settings to avoid damage. Similarly, the type of graffiti (e.g., spray paint, marker, or etching) and the length of time it has been on the surface can impact the removal process.

Selecting the Right Equipment and Cleaning Solutions

To effectively remove graffiti, you'll need a power washer with a high enough pressure setting to loosen and remove the paint or other substance. A pressure setting of at least 3000 psi is typically recommended for graffiti removal, along with a narrow-angle nozzle (15 or 25 degrees) for concentrated cleaning power.

In addition to the power washer itself, you may need to use specialized cleaning solutions designed for graffiti removal. These solutions often contain solvents or other chemicals that help to break down and dissolve the graffiti, making it easier to remove with the power washer. Be sure to choose a cleaning solution that is appropriate for the type of surface you are cleaning and follow the manufacturer's instructions for application and use.

Techniques for Removing Graffiti

1. Test a small area first

Before applying any cleaning solution or beginning to power wash, test a small, inconspicuous area of the surface to ensure that the cleaning method won't cause any damage or discoloration.

2. Apply cleaning solution

If using a cleaning solution, apply it to the graffiti according to the manufacturer's instructions. Allow the solution to dwell on the surface for the recommended amount of time to penetrate and loosen the graffiti.

3. Power wash the surface

Using the appropriate pressure setting and nozzle, begin power washing the surface, starting at the top of the graffiti and working your way down. Use a consistent, overlapping motion to ensure that all areas of the graffiti are treated evenly.

4. Adjust techniques as needed
If the graffiti is not coming off easily, you may need to adjust your pressure setting, nozzle angle, or cleaning solution. Be patient and persistent, as some types of graffiti may require multiple passes or additional soaking time to fully remove.

5. Rinse thoroughly
Once the graffiti has been removed, rinse the surface thoroughly with clean water to remove any remaining cleaning solution or debris.

Preventing Future Graffiti

While power washing can be an effective way to remove graffiti, it's also important to take steps to prevent future occurrences. Consider the following strategies:

1. Apply anti-graffiti coatings
Specialized anti-graffiti coatings can be applied to surfaces to make it easier to remove graffiti in the future. These coatings create a barrier between the surface and the graffiti, allowing for easier removal without damaging the underlying material.

2. Install lighting and surveillance
Improving lighting and installing surveillance cameras in areas prone to graffiti can help to deter vandals and make it easier to identify and prosecute offenders.

3. Encourage community involvement
Engaging the community in graffiti prevention and removal efforts can help to create a sense of ownership and pride in the area, discouraging future vandalism.

By understanding the techniques and considerations involved in graffiti removal, you can expand your power washing skills and take on more advanced cleaning projects. Remember to always prioritize safety and carefully assess each situation to determine the most appropriate and effective approach.

Whether you are a homeowner looking to maintain a clean and inviting property or a business owner seeking to create a professional and welcoming environment, the ability to effectively remove graffiti and other challenging stains and debris is a valuable skill. With the right knowledge, equipment, and techniques, you can tackle even the toughest power washing projects with confidence and achieve outstanding results.

Rust and Oil Stain Removal

Rust and oil stains are common issues that can be challenging to remove from various surfaces. These stubborn stains not only detract from the appearance of a surface but can also lead to further damage if left untreated. Power washing can be an effective method for removing rust and oil stains, but it requires specific techniques and cleaning solutions to achieve the best results. In this section, we'll delve into the process of rust and oil stain removal using power washing.

Understanding Rust and Oil Stains

Rust stains occur when metal objects containing iron are exposed to moisture and oxygen, causing a chemical reaction that results in the formation of iron oxide, or rust. This reddish-brown substance can easily transfer to surfaces like concrete, brick, or stone, leaving behind unsightly stains.

Oil stains, on the other hand, are caused by the accumulation of grease, automotive fluids, or other oily substances on a surface. These stains can be particularly stubborn on porous materials like concrete, where the oil can seep deep into the surface.

Preparing for Rust and Oil Stain Removal

Before attempting to remove rust or oil stains with a power washer, it's essential to properly prepare the area and gather the necessary equipment and cleaning solutions.

1. Clear the area: Remove any objects or debris from the surface to be cleaned, ensuring that you have clear access to the stained areas.

2. Protect surrounding surfaces: If there are any nearby surfaces or objects that could be damaged by the power washing process, cover them with tarps or plastic sheeting to protect them from overspray or runoff.

3. Choose the right cleaning solutions: Select a cleaning solution specifically designed for removing rust or oil stains, depending on the type of stain you are dealing with. These specialized solutions often contain surfactants, solvents, or other chemicals that help to break down and lift the stains from the surface.

4. Select appropriate power washer settings: Choose a power washer with a pressure setting of at least 2000 psi for most rust and oil stain removal projects. A narrow-angle nozzle (15 or 25 degrees) can help to concentrate the cleaning power on the stained areas.

Removing Rust Stains

1. Apply cleaning solution: Following the manufacturer's instructions, apply the rust-removal cleaning solution to the stained area. Allow the solution to dwell on the surface for the recommended amount of time to penetrate and loosen the rust stains.

2. Power wash the surface: Using the appropriate pressure setting and nozzle, begin power washing the stained area, starting at the edges of the stain and working your way inward. Use a consistent, overlapping motion to ensure even coverage.

3. Adjust techniques as needed: If the rust stains are not coming off easily, you may need to adjust your pressure setting, nozzle angle, or apply additional cleaning solution. Be patient and persistent, as some rust stains may require multiple passes to fully remove.

4. Rinse thoroughly: Once the rust stains have been removed, rinse the surface thoroughly with clean water to remove any remaining cleaning solution or debris.

Removing Oil Stains

1. Pre-treat the stain: Before applying the cleaning solution, pre-treat the oil stain with a degreaser or oil-absorbing product, such as cat litter or baking soda. Allow the pre-treatment to sit on the stain for the recommended amount of time to absorb excess oil.

2. Apply cleaning solution: After pre-treating the stain, apply the oil-removal cleaning solution to the affected area, following the manufacturer's instructions. Allow the solution to dwell on the surface for the recommended time to penetrate and emulsify the oil.

3. Power wash the surface: Using the appropriate pressure setting and nozzle, begin power washing the stained area, starting at the edges of the stain and working your way inward. Use a consistent, overlapping motion to ensure even coverage.

4. Adjust techniques as needed: If the oil stains are not coming off easily, you may need to adjust your pressure setting, nozzle angle, or apply additional cleaning solution. Some oil stains may require multiple passes or additional dwell time to fully remove.

5. Rinse thoroughly: Once the oil stains have been removed, rinse the surface thoroughly with clean water to remove any remaining cleaning solution or debris.

Preventing Rust and Oil Stains

To minimize the occurrence of rust and oil stains on your surfaces, consider the following prevention strategies:

1. Seal porous surfaces: Apply a sealant to porous surfaces like concrete to create a barrier that prevents rust and oil from penetrating the material.

2. Address sources of stains: Identify and address any sources of rust or oil stains, such as leaking machinery or vehicles, to prevent future staining.

3. Clean up spills promptly: If a spill occurs, clean it up as quickly as possible to prevent the substance from penetrating and staining the surface.

By understanding the specific techniques and considerations involved in rust and oil stain removal, you can effectively tackle these challenging cleaning projects with your power washer. Always prioritize safety and carefully follow the instructions provided by the cleaning solution manufacturer to achieve the best results.

Remember, the key to successful stain removal is patience, persistence, and the right combination of equipment, cleaning solutions, and techniques. With practice and experience, you'll be able to confidently take on even the toughest rust and oil stains, restoring your surfaces to their original beauty and protecting them from future damage.

Preparing Surfaces for Painting or Staining

Before applying a fresh coat of paint or stain to any surface, proper preparation is crucial to ensure optimal results and long-lasting durability. Power washing can be an effective method for cleaning and preparing surfaces for painting or staining, as it removes dirt, grime, loose paint, and other contaminants that could interfere with adhesion or cause a subpar finish. In this section, we'll explore the process of using power washing to prepare surfaces for painting or staining.

Assessing the Surface

The first step in preparing a surface for painting or staining is to assess its current condition and identify any issues that need to be addressed before proceeding. Some common problems to look for include:

1. Loose or peeling paint
2. Cracks or holes in the surface
3. Mold, mildew, or algae growth
4. Rust or corrosion (on metal surfaces)
5. Grease or oil stains
6. Efflorescence (white, powdery deposits on masonry surfaces)

Make note of any areas that require special attention or repair before power washing and subsequent painting or staining.

Gathering Necessary Equipment and Supplies

To effectively prepare a surface for painting or staining using power washing, you'll need the following equipment and supplies:

1. Power washer with adjustable pressure settings and interchangeable nozzles
2. Appropriate cleaning solution for the type of surface and contaminants present
3. Safety gear (eye protection, gloves, etc.)
4. Drop cloths or tarps to protect surrounding areas
5. Scrub brush or sponge for manual cleaning (if needed)
6. Sandpaper or wire brush for removing loose paint or rust
7. Putty knife or patching compound for filling cracks or holes

Preparing the Area

Before beginning the power washing process, take steps to protect the surrounding area and any items that could be damaged by overspray or runoff:

1. Remove or cover outdoor furniture, potted plants, and decorations
2. Tape off or cover windows, doors, and electrical outlets
3. Place drop cloths or tarps on the ground and over nearby vegetation
4. Ensure proper ventilation if working in an enclosed space

Power Washing the Surface

Once the area is prepared, follow these steps to power wash the surface:

1. Select the appropriate pressure setting and nozzle for the type of surface and contaminants present. A lower pressure setting (1200-1800 psi) and a wider nozzle (25-40 degrees) are generally recommended for preparing surfaces for painting or staining to avoid damaging the substrate.

2. Test the power washer on an inconspicuous area to ensure the pressure setting and nozzle are appropriate and not causing any damage.

3. Apply the cleaning solution, if using one, according to the manufacturer's instructions. Allow the solution to dwell on the surface for the recommended time to help loosen dirt and contaminants.

4. Begin power washing the surface, starting at the top and working your way down to prevent streaking. Use overlapping strokes and maintain a consistent distance from the surface to ensure even cleaning.

5. Pay extra attention to heavily soiled or stained areas, using a scrub brush or sponge to agitate the surface if needed.

6. Rinse the surface thoroughly with clean water to remove any remaining cleaning solution and debris.

Repairing and Sanding the Surface

After power washing, allow the surface to dry completely, then inspect it for any remaining issues that need to be addressed before painting or staining:

1. Scrape away any loose or peeling paint using a putty knife or wire brush.
2. Fill any cracks or holes with patching compound, following the manufacturer's instructions for application and drying time.
3. Sand the surface lightly to create a smooth, even substrate for the new paint or stain to adhere to. Use a fine-grit sandpaper (120-150 grit) and sand in the direction of the wood grain, if applicable.

4. Remove any dust or debris from sanding using a tack cloth or damp rag.

Final Preparations

Before applying the new paint or stain, take these final steps to ensure the best possible results:

1. Ensure the surface is completely clean and dry.
2. Apply painter's tape to any edges, trim, or adjacent surfaces you want to protect from the paint or stain.
3. If using a primer, apply it according to the manufacturer's instructions and allow it to dry completely before proceeding with the paint or stain.

By following these steps and taking the time to properly prepare your surface using power washing and other necessary techniques, you'll create an ideal foundation for your new paint or stain. This will result in a more attractive, even finish that will better withstand the elements and regular wear and tear over time.

Remember, the success of any painting or staining project depends largely on the quality of the surface preparation. By investing the time and effort to clean, repair, and prime your surface correctly, you'll be able to achieve professional-looking results that you can be proud of for years to come.

Chapter 7
hiring a Professional Power Washing Service

When to Consider Professional Help

While power washing can be a rewarding DIY project, there are times when it may be more appropriate to hire a professional power washing service. Professional power washers have the experience, equipment, and expertise to tackle even the most challenging cleaning projects efficiently and effectively, ensuring optimal results and minimizing the risk of damage to your property. In this section, we'll discuss when to consider professional help and what to expect from a professional power washing service.

When to Consider Professional Help

There are several situations where hiring a professional power washing service may be the best choice:

1. Large or complex projects: If you have a particularly large or complex power washing project, such as a multi-story home or a large commercial property, it may be more practical and time-efficient to hire professionals to handle the job.

2. Lack of experience or equipment: If you are new to power washing or don't have access to the necessary equipment, it may be safer and more effective to leave the job to professionals who have the knowledge and tools to achieve the best results.

3. Safety concerns: Power washing can be dangerous, especially when working on elevated surfaces or with high-pressure equipment. If you have any concerns about your ability to safely complete the project, it's best to hire professionals who are trained and experienced in using power washing equipment safely.

4. Delicate or historic surfaces: If you need to clean delicate or historic surfaces, such as old brick or soft stone, it's important to use the correct techniques and pressure settings to avoid causing damage. Professional power washers have the knowledge and experience to clean these surfaces safely and effectively.

5. Stubborn stains or contaminants: Some stains or contaminants, such as heavy mildew growth or oil stains, can be particularly challenging to remove. Professional power washers have access to specialized cleaning solutions and techniques that can effectively tackle these stubborn issues.

6. Time constraints: If you have a tight deadline for completing your power washing project, such as preparing for a special event or a real estate showing, hiring professionals can help ensure the job is completed on time and to a high standard.

Choosing a Reputable Power Washing Company

When selecting a professional power washing company, it's essential to do your research and choose a reputable, experienced provider. Consider the following factors:

1. Experience: Look for a company with a proven track record of successfully completing projects similar to yours. Ask about their experience with your specific type of surface or stain.

2. Equipment and techniques: Inquire about the equipment and techniques the company uses to ensure they are up-to-date and appropriate for your project. A reputable company should be able to explain their process and why it's the best approach for your needs.

3. Insurance and licensing: Verify that the company is properly insured and licensed to operate in your area. This protects you in case of any accidents or damage that may occur during the power washing process.

4. References and reviews: Ask for references from past clients and check online reviews to get a sense of the company's reputation and the quality of their work.

5. Price and value: While it's important to get a competitive price, be wary of companies that offer rates significantly lower than others, as this may be a sign of subpar equipment, techniques, or insurance coverage. Look for a company that provides a fair price and value for their services.

What to Expect from Professional Power Washing Services

When you hire a professional power washing company, you can expect the following:

1. Comprehensive assessment: A professional will assess your property and the surfaces to be cleaned, identifying any potential challenges or special considerations.

2. Customized plan: Based on the assessment, the company will develop a customized plan for your project, including the appropriate equipment, techniques, and cleaning solutions to use.

3. Preparation and protection: The power washing team will take steps to prepare and protect your property, such as covering landscaping, moving outdoor furniture, and taping off doors and windows.

4. Efficient and effective cleaning: Using their expertise and professional-grade equipment, the power washing team will efficiently and effectively clean your surfaces, taking care to address any stubborn stains or contaminants.

5. Thorough cleanup: After the power washing is complete, the team will thoroughly clean up the work area, leaving your property tidy and ready to enjoy.

6. Follow-up and maintenance: A reputable power washing company will provide recommendations for maintaining your newly cleaned surfaces and may offer ongoing maintenance services to keep your property looking its best.

By understanding when to consider professional help and what to expect from a professional power washing service, you can make an informed decision about the best approach for your specific needs. Whether you choose to tackle the project yourself or hire a professional, the goal is to achieve a clean, well-maintained property that you can be proud of.

Choosing a Reputable Power Washing Company

When it comes to ensuring the best results for your power washing project, selecting a reputable and experienced professional is crucial. A reliable power washing company will have the knowledge, equipment, and skills necessary to effectively clean your surfaces while minimizing the risk of damage. In this section, we'll delve into the key factors to consider when choosing a reputable power washing company.

1. Experience and Expertise

One of the most important aspects to consider when selecting a power washing company is their level of experience and expertise. Look for a company with a proven track record of successfully completing projects similar to yours. Experienced professionals will have the knowledge and skills to tackle a wide range of surfaces and stains, and they'll be able to provide valuable insights and recommendations based on their expertise.

When evaluating a company's experience, consider the following:

- Years in business
- Types of projects they have completed
- Specialized training or certifications
- Familiarity with your specific type of surface or stain

2. Equipment and Techniques

A reputable power washing company should use high-quality, well-maintained equipment and up-to-date techniques to ensure optimal results. Inquire about the specific equipment and methods they use, and make sure they are appropriate for your project.

Some key equipment and techniques to ask about include:

- Pressure washers (hot water or cold water)
- Nozzle types and sizes
- Cleaning solutions and detergents
- Surface-specific techniques (e.g., soft washing for delicate surfaces)
- Eco-friendly or low-impact options

A knowledgeable and transparent company should be able to explain their equipment and techniques in detail and provide a rationale for their approach.

3. Insurance and Licensing

Proper insurance and licensing are essential for protecting yourself and your property in case of any accidents or damage during the power washing process. Always verify that the company you are considering is fully insured and licensed to operate in your area.

Types of insurance to look for include:

- General liability insurance
- Workers' compensation insurance
- Property damage insurance

Licensing requirements may vary by location, so be sure to check with your local authorities to ensure the company meets all necessary regulations.

4. References and Reviews

One of the best ways to gauge the quality and reliability of a power washing company is to hear from their past clients. Ask the company for references, and take the time to contact these individuals to ask about their experience, the quality of the work, and their overall satisfaction.

In addition to references, check online review platforms like Google, Yelp, or HomeAdvisor to see what others are saying about the company. Pay attention to both positive and negative reviews, and look for patterns or common themes that may indicate the company's strengths or weaknesses.

5. Price and Value

While cost is certainly a factor when choosing a power washing company, it's important not to base your decision solely on price. Extremely low prices may be a red flag, indicating subpar equipment, inadequate insurance, or lack of experience.

Instead, look for a company that provides a fair and competitive price while also delivering exceptional value. This may include:

- Detailed, transparent quotes
- Customized solutions for your specific needs
- High-quality equipment and cleaning solutions
- Experienced, knowledgeable technicians
- Excellent customer service and communication
- Satisfaction guarantees or warranties

6. Professionalism and Communication

Finally, pay attention to the overall professionalism and communication skills of the power washing company. From your initial inquiry to the completion of the project, the company should be responsive, informative, and courteous.

Some signs of a professional and communicative company include:

- Prompt and clear responses to your questions or concerns
- Detailed, written estimates and contracts
- Open communication about their processes, timeline, and any potential issues
- Respect for your property and privacy
- Punctuality and reliability
- Professional appearance and demeanor

By carefully evaluating these key factors, you can feel confident in choosing a reputable power washing company that will deliver exceptional results while providing a positive, stress-free experience. Remember, taking the time to research and select the right professional will pay off in the long run, ensuring your surfaces are properly cleaned and maintained for years to come.

What to Expect from Professional Power Washing Services

When you hire a professional power washing company, you can expect a comprehensive, efficient, and effective cleaning experience that delivers exceptional results. A reputable power washing service will take the time to understand your unique needs, develop a customized plan, and execute the project with skill and attention to detail. In this section, we'll explore what you can expect from professional power washing services, from the initial consultation to the final walkthrough.

1. Comprehensive Assessment

The first step in any professional power washing project is a thorough assessment of your property and the surfaces to be cleaned. During this initial consultation, a knowledgeable technician will visit your site to evaluate the condition of your surfaces, identify any potential challenges or concerns, and gather the necessary information to develop a tailored cleaning plan.

The assessment may include:

- Identifying the type and condition of surfaces to be cleaned
- Noting any areas of heavy soiling, staining, or damage
- Assessing accessibility and safety considerations
- Determining the appropriate equipment, techniques, and cleaning solutions
- Discussing your specific goals and expectations for the project

2. Customized Plan

Based on the comprehensive assessment, the power washing company will develop a customized plan for your project. This plan will outline the specific steps, equipment, and techniques necessary to achieve optimal results while minimizing the risk of damage to your surfaces.

A well-designed power washing plan may include:

- Specific pressure settings and nozzle types for each surface
- Appropriate cleaning solutions and dwell times
- Surface-specific techniques (e.g., soft washing for delicate surfaces)
- Safety measures and precautions
- Timeline and sequence of cleaning tasks
- Pricing and payment details

The company should review the plan with you in detail, answering any questions you may have and making any necessary adjustments based on your feedback.

3. Preparation and Protection

Before beginning the actual power washing process, the professional team will take steps to prepare your property and protect any areas that are not to be cleaned. This preparation phase is crucial for ensuring a safe and efficient cleaning process while minimizing the risk of damage.

Preparation and protection measures may include:

- Covering or moving outdoor furniture, potted plants, and decorations

- Taping off or shielding windows, doors, and electrical outlets
- Placing drop cloths or tarps on the ground and over nearby vegetation
- Securing any loose items that could be blown away by the high-pressure water
- Ensuring proper ventilation if working in an enclosed space
- Setting up safety barriers or signage to keep people and pets away from the work area

4. Efficient and Effective Cleaning

With the preparation complete, the power washing team will begin the core cleaning process. Using their expertise and professional-grade equipment, they will systematically clean your surfaces, paying close attention to heavily soiled or stained areas.

The cleaning process may involve:

- Applying cleaning solutions and allowing appropriate dwell times
- Using the proper pressure settings and nozzle types for each surface
- Employing surface-specific techniques like soft washing or hot water washing
- Adjusting techniques or products as needed based on the surface's response
- Thoroughly rinsing surfaces to remove cleaning solutions and debris
- Inspecting surfaces for any missed spots or areas requiring additional attention

Throughout the cleaning process, the team will work efficiently to minimize disruption to your property while ensuring a thorough, effective clean.

5. Thorough Cleanup

Once the power washing is complete, the professional team will conduct a thorough cleanup of the work area. This involves removing any protective coverings, collecting any debris or waste generated during the cleaning process, and returning your property to its original condition.

Cleanup tasks may include:

- Removing drop cloths, tarps, and protective tape
- Collecting and disposing of any debris or waste
- Wiping down any surfaces that may have been splashed or overspray
- Returning outdoor furniture, plants, and decorations to their original positions
- Conducting a final inspection to ensure the work area is tidy and secure

6. Final Walkthrough and Follow-Up

After the cleaning and cleanup are complete, the power washing company will typically conduct a final walkthrough with you to review the results and ensure your satisfaction. This is an opportunity for you to inspect the cleaned surfaces, ask any remaining questions, and provide feedback on the overall experience.

During the final walkthrough, the company may:

- Guide you through the cleaned areas, pointing out any notable improvements
- Explain any challenges encountered during the process and how they were addressed

- Provide recommendations for maintaining your newly cleaned surfaces
- Offer ongoing maintenance services to keep your property looking its best
- Address any concerns or questions you may have
- Collect final payment and provide any necessary documentation

Following the walkthrough, a reputable power washing company will follow up with you to ensure your continued satisfaction and address any issues that may arise.

By understanding what to expect from professional power washing services, you can make an informed decision when selecting a company and feel confident in the quality and value of the services you receive. A reputable power washing company will prioritize your needs, communicate clearly, and deliver exceptional results, leaving you with beautifully cleaned and well-maintained surfaces that enhance the appearance and value of your property.

-

Conclusion

Congratulations on making it to the end of this comprehensive guide on power washing! By now, you should have a thorough understanding of the many benefits, techniques, and applications of this powerful cleaning method.

Throughout this book, we've explored the transformative potential of power washing, from restoring the beauty of your home's exterior to maintaining the integrity and value of your property. We've covered the essential tools and equipment needed for success, as well as the important safety precautions to keep in mind when working with high-pressure water.

You've learned how to tackle a wide range of surfaces, from delicate siding and wood to sturdy concrete and masonry. We've delved into advanced applications like graffiti removal and oil stain elimination, empowering you with the knowledge and skills to take on even the toughest cleaning challenges.

But beyond the technical aspects of power washing, we've also emphasized the importance of eco-friendly and sustainable practices. By using biodegradable cleaning solutions, conserving water, and properly disposing of wastewater and debris, you can enjoy the benefits of a clean and beautiful property while minimizing your environmental impact.

As you embark on your own power washing projects, remember the key principles of preparation, technique, and safety. Take the time to assess your surfaces, choose the right equipment and products, and work methodically to achieve the best possible results. And don't be afraid to seek professional help when needed – a reputable power washing company can provide the expertise and resources to tackle even the most complex jobs.

Above all, embrace the transformative power of power washing. Whether you're revitalizing your home's curb appeal, preparing surfaces for a fresh coat of paint, or simply maintaining a clean and inviting outdoor space, power washing is a valuable tool in your property maintenance arsenal.

So go forth and harness the power of water pressure! With the knowledge and techniques you've gained from this book, you're well-equipped to tackle any power washing project that comes your way. Happy cleaning!

Made in the USA
Middletown, DE
12 July 2025